Discover & Learn

United Kingdom

This book is for pupils studying the UK
in KS2 Geography (ages 7-11).

It's packed with facts, maps and questions covering
locational knowledge of the United Kingdom — ideal
for exploring and understanding the whole topic.

Published by CGP

Consultant: Joanna Copley

Editors: Mary Falkner, Sharon Keeley-Holden, Sarah Pattison, Rebecca Russell

Reviewer: Alison Griffin

ISBN: 978 1 78294 979 4

With thanks to David Ryan for the proofreading.

With thanks to Jan Greenway for the copyright research.

Printed by Elanders Ltd, Newcastle upon Tyne

Clipart from Corel®

Contents

Meet the UK

The UK is short for "<u>The United Kingdom of Great Britain and Northern Ireland</u>". It's made up of <u>four</u> different countries that are joined together, or 'united'.

The four countries that make up the UK are <u>England</u>, <u>Scotland</u>, <u>Wales</u> and <u>Northern Ireland</u>. Each country has a capital city. The four countries and their capitals are shown on this map.

Fact Sheet: Northern Ireland

Area: About 14 000 square kilometres (about 5500 square miles).

Population: About 2 million

Capital city: Belfast

Did you know? Lough Neagh in Northern Ireland is the largest lake in the UK.

The bit of the map shown in grey here is the country of Ireland. It isn't part of the UK.

If you could live anywhere in the UK, where would you choose? Why?

Fact Sheet: Wales

Area: About 21 000 square kilometres (about 8000 square miles).

Population: About 3 million

Capital city: Cardiff

Did you know? Wales has its own language. About 20% of people in Wales can speak Welsh.

A country of islands...

The biggest island in the UK is called "Great Britain". Great Britain makes up more than three quarters of the total area of the UK.

But there are more than a thousand smaller islands that are part of the UK too. Here are some of the islands that make up the UK:

Fact Sheet: Scotland

Area: About 80 000 square kilometres (about 30 000 square miles).

Population: About 5.5 million

Capital city: Edinburgh

Did you know? The highest mountain in the UK is Ben Nevis. It's in Western Scotland and it's 1345 m high.

Fact Sheet: England

Area: About 130 000 square kilometres (about 50 000 square miles).

Population: About 55 million

Capital city: London

Did you know? The tallest building in the UK is The Shard in London — it's about 310 m high.

Here, there and everywhere...

Even though the UK is made up of different countries there's no border control. That means everyone can freely travel from country to country within the UK.

The Organisation of the UK

There are many decisions that have to be made to help a country run smoothly.
The countries of the UK all have a say in how some things are run.

Who makes the rules?

Each of the countries in the UK has a parliament building.
This is where the government of that country meets to make the laws for the country.

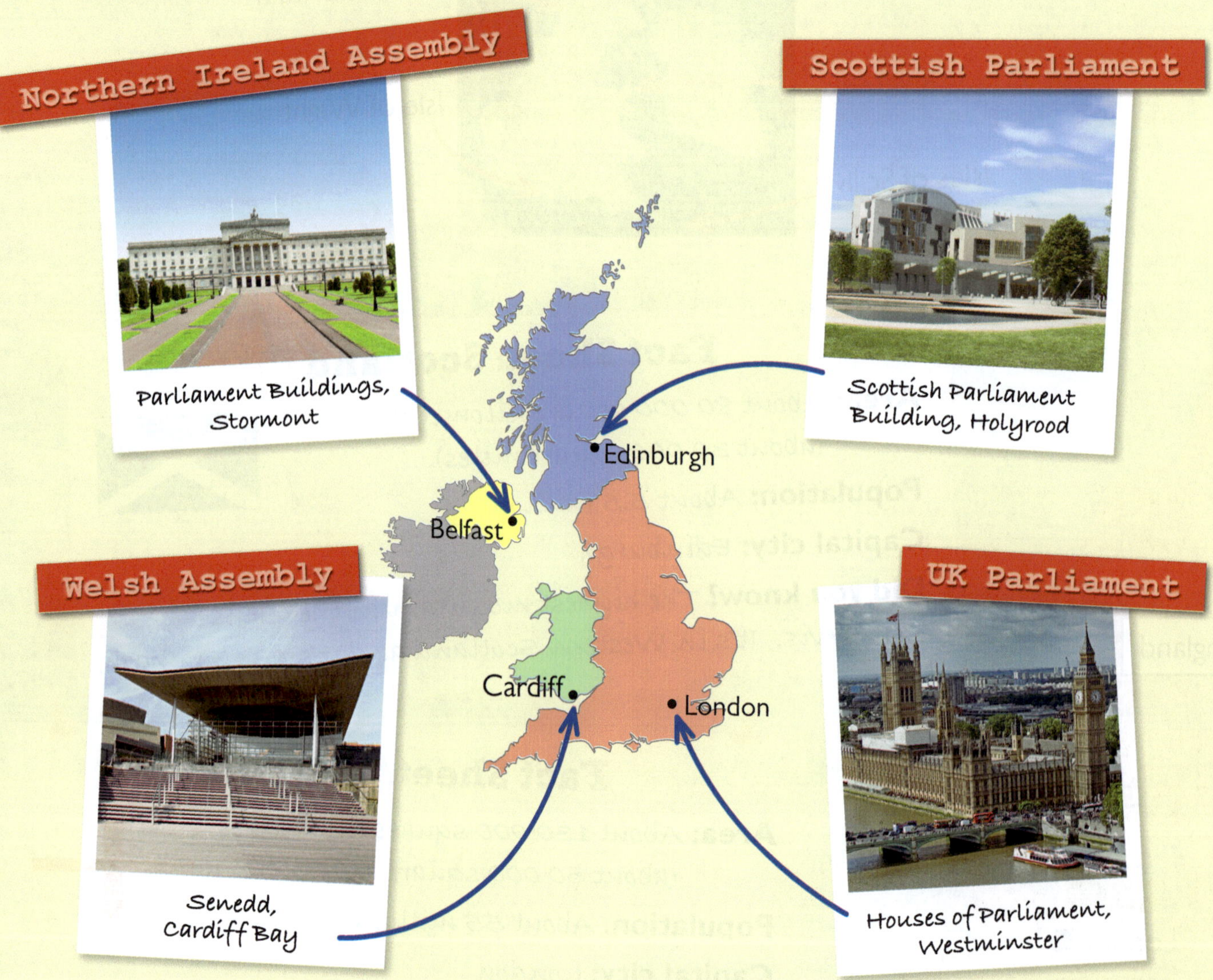

The UK Parliament makes laws that affect the whole of the United Kingdom.

The Scottish Parliament, Welsh Assembly and the Northern Ireland Assembly make laws that only affect their own part of the UK.

The UK government controls things like the army, trade and relationships with other countries. Services like the health service and education are controlled by each country's own government.

A patchwork country...

Each country of the UK is split up into <u>smaller</u> areas that decide how to run things <u>locally</u>.

In England these smaller areas are called <u>counties</u> and in Northern Ireland they are <u>districts</u>.
In Wales they are called <u>principal areas</u> and in Scotland they're known as <u>council areas</u>.

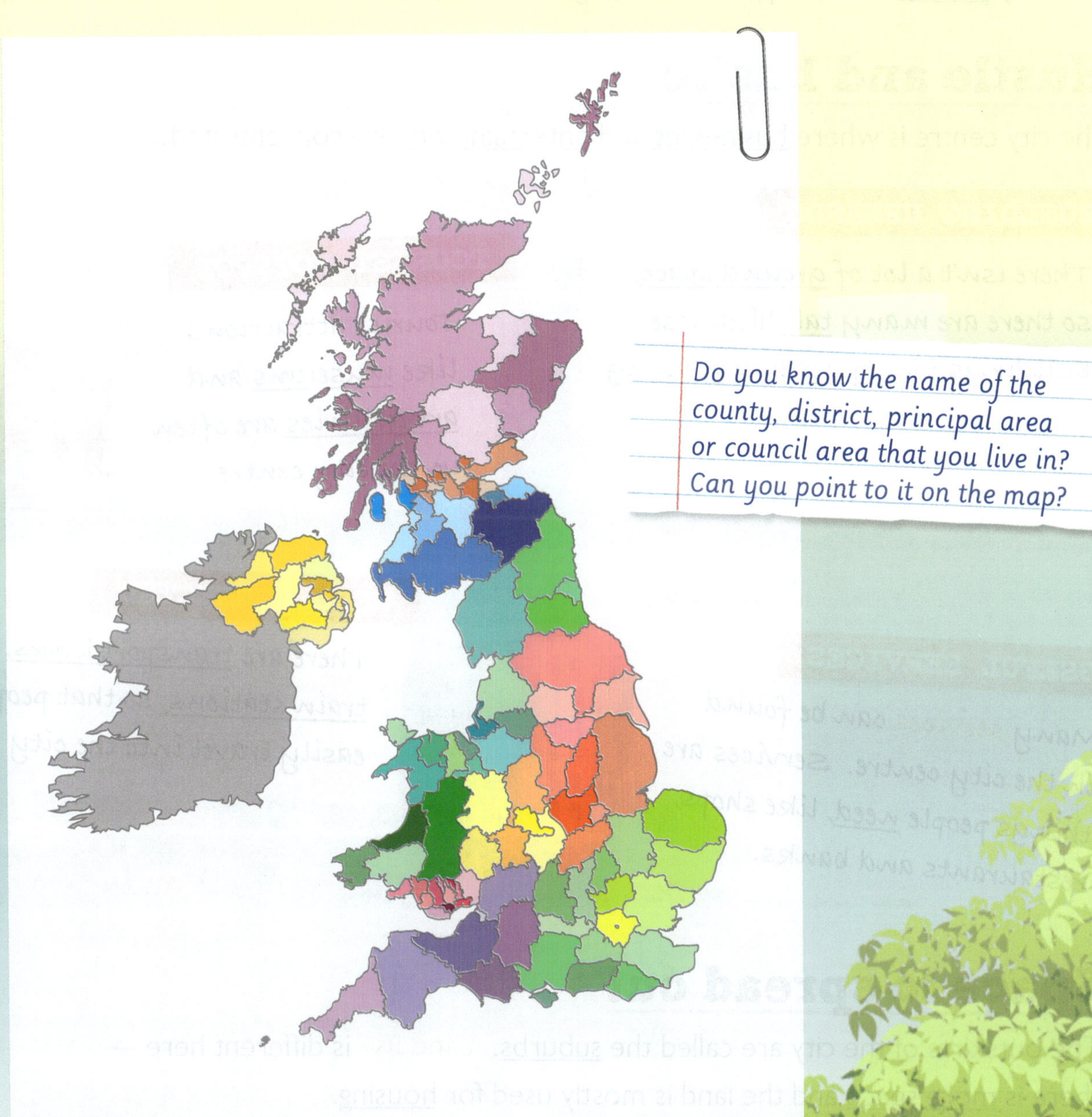

These areas of the UK have their own <u>local governments</u>.
A local government is in charge of making decisions about issues in the <u>local area</u>,
which can include things like how <u>schools</u> are run and where to improve <u>roads</u>.

All shapes and sizes...

The areas that local governments are in charge of vary a lot in size. Highland in Scotland
is almost 10,000 times bigger than the smallest county in the UK, the City of London.

In the City

A city is a very large settlement. Many people live and work in cities. The centre of a city is usually packed with people and buildings, but away from the centre there is more space.

Hustle and bustle

The city centre is where businesses and entertainment are concentrated...

BUILDING UPWARDS

There isn't a lot of ground space, so there are many tall high-rise buildings for offices and housing.

TOURIST HOTSPOT

Tourist attractions like museums and art galleries are often in the city centre.

USEFUL SERVICES

Many services can be found in the city centre. Services are things people need, like shops, restaurants and banks.

WELL CONNECTED

There are transport links, like train stations, so that people can easily travel into the city centre.

Space to spread out

The outskirts of the city are called the suburbs. Land use is different here — there is more space and the land is mostly used for housing.

Outside the centre, you often find services that need more space, like large hospitals, airports, golf courses and large supermarkets.

You also find factories, larger office buildings and motorways.

Homes here are usually bigger and further apart than those close to the centre.

Let's look at a city...

Birmingham is Britain's second biggest city. It is a huge urban area with a population of over one million. The OS® map below shows some of it. The key on the inside back cover of this book shows you what the different symbols mean.

Birmingham

In the centre of Birmingham is the 'Bullring' — a huge shopping and business area. It is visited by tourists as well as local people.

The Bullring

Do you think it is good to have lots of shops close together in one central area? Why or why not?

What differences in land use can you see between the centre and the outskirts of Birmingham?

On the outskirts of Birmingham is the airport. An airport needs lots of space for the terminal buildings, runway and car parks.

What types of transport can you see going into the city centre?.

Birmingham Airport

City centres – skyscrapers, sirens and shops...

Every so often, the Government and the King pick some towns to become new cities. In the past, towns couldn't become cities unless they had a cathedral, and some cities were rather teeny. Nowadays, it's mostly the biggest towns that become cities.

In the Country

Only a <u>small</u> amount of the land in the UK is <u>urban</u> — most of it is <u>rural</u>.
The land in rural areas is mainly used for agriculture (farming).

Down on the farm...

How farmland is used depends on the <u>climate</u> (what the <u>weather</u> is mostly like) and
what the <u>ground</u> is like (whether it is <u>rocky hills</u> or <u>rich soil</u>). Some farms are <u>mixed</u>
— they are used for more than one type of farming.

CATTLE FARMING

<u>Warm</u>, <u>wet</u> places have rich <u>grass</u> which is perfect for cattle farming. These farms produce <u>meat</u> and <u>dairy products</u>, like milk.

HILL FARMING

<u>Hilly</u> places can be a bit <u>chilly</u> and the <u>grass</u> is often poor. They're no good for other sorts of farming, so they are often used for <u>sheep</u>.

ARABLE FARMING

Land with <u>good soil</u> is used for arable farming (growing crops). <u>Flat</u> land is needed so <u>machinery</u> like combine harvesters can be used.

Farming is an economic activity — farmers make <u>money</u> by selling the food and other things they produce.

Rocky hills, flat fields or lush grass

Different regions of the UK have different <u>climates</u> and <u>soils</u>. Some regions have <u>steep hills</u> but others are <u>flat</u>. This means that farmland in each region is <u>used differently</u>.

Not everyone who lives in the countryside is a farmer

Some people who live in the countryside work on farms, and others have jobs connected with farming, e.g. in animal feed factories. However, plenty of people who live in the countryside have jobs in schools, shops, police stations and doctors' surgeries in the area. Many other people commute (travel) to nearby towns and cities everyday to go to work.

Changes in Land Use

Most of the land in the UK is used by people for <u>something</u>, like <u>farming</u>, <u>housing</u> or <u>leisure</u>.
But the way it is used <u>changes over time</u>...

Scarborough – 1880

This map shows the town of <u>Scarborough</u>, North Yorkshire in 1880.

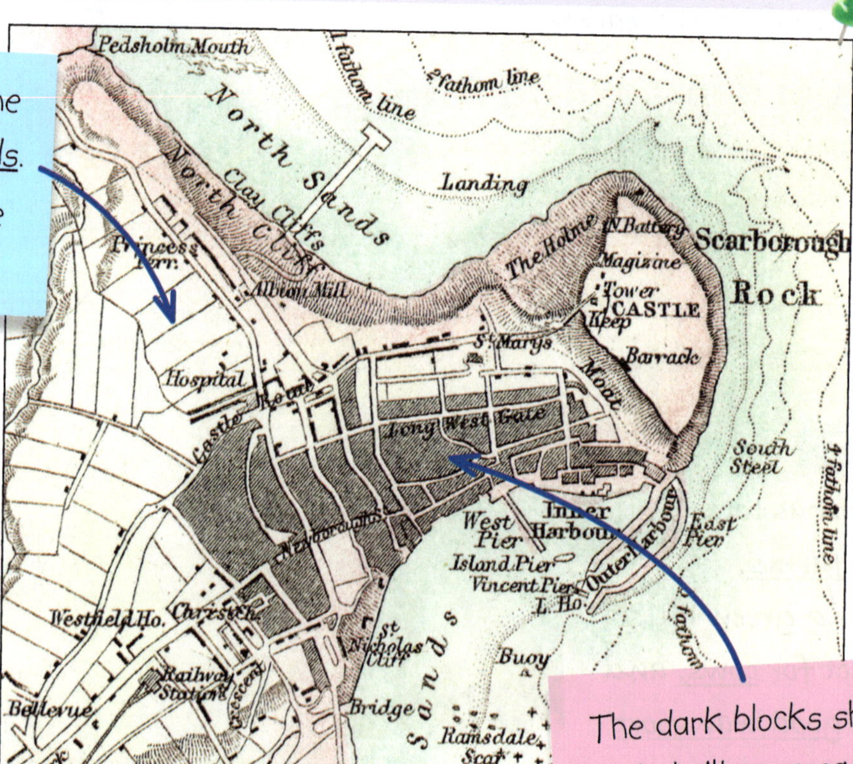

Thin black lines show the <u>boundaries</u> between <u>fields</u>.
These fields would have been used for <u>farming</u>.

The dark blocks show the main <u>built-up areas</u> of the town. Tiny black squares also show <u>individual buildings</u>.

In 1880, Scarborough was a small <u>fishing</u> town that had already become a popular seaside <u>holiday resort</u>. Tourists often came to enjoy the lovely <u>beaches</u> or to drink <u>spa water</u> (which was supposed to make people healthier).

Can you see anything else on the map you think tourists might have wanted to visit?

Scarborough – 2018

Below is an Ordnance Survey® map of the town in 2018. In some places the land use has <u>changed</u> — but in others it <u>hasn't</u>. Start off by looking at the map below, then have a go at the questions on this page.

If you don't know what these things look like on an OS map, have a look at the key on the inside of the back cover of this book.

Compare this map to the map on the previous page. What has happened to the number of roads since 1880?

Are there more or fewer fields now than there were in 1880? Can you spot anything that has stayed the same since 1880?

Do you think other towns will have changed over time in similar ways? What types of land use do you think stay the same for a long time?

What we need from the land is always changing...

Land use in cities and in rural areas is always changing. New houses and businesses are built, forests can be turned into farmland and farmland can be turned into housing.

North Eastern England

The <u>counties</u> and some <u>large cities</u> in North Eastern England are labelled on the map below.

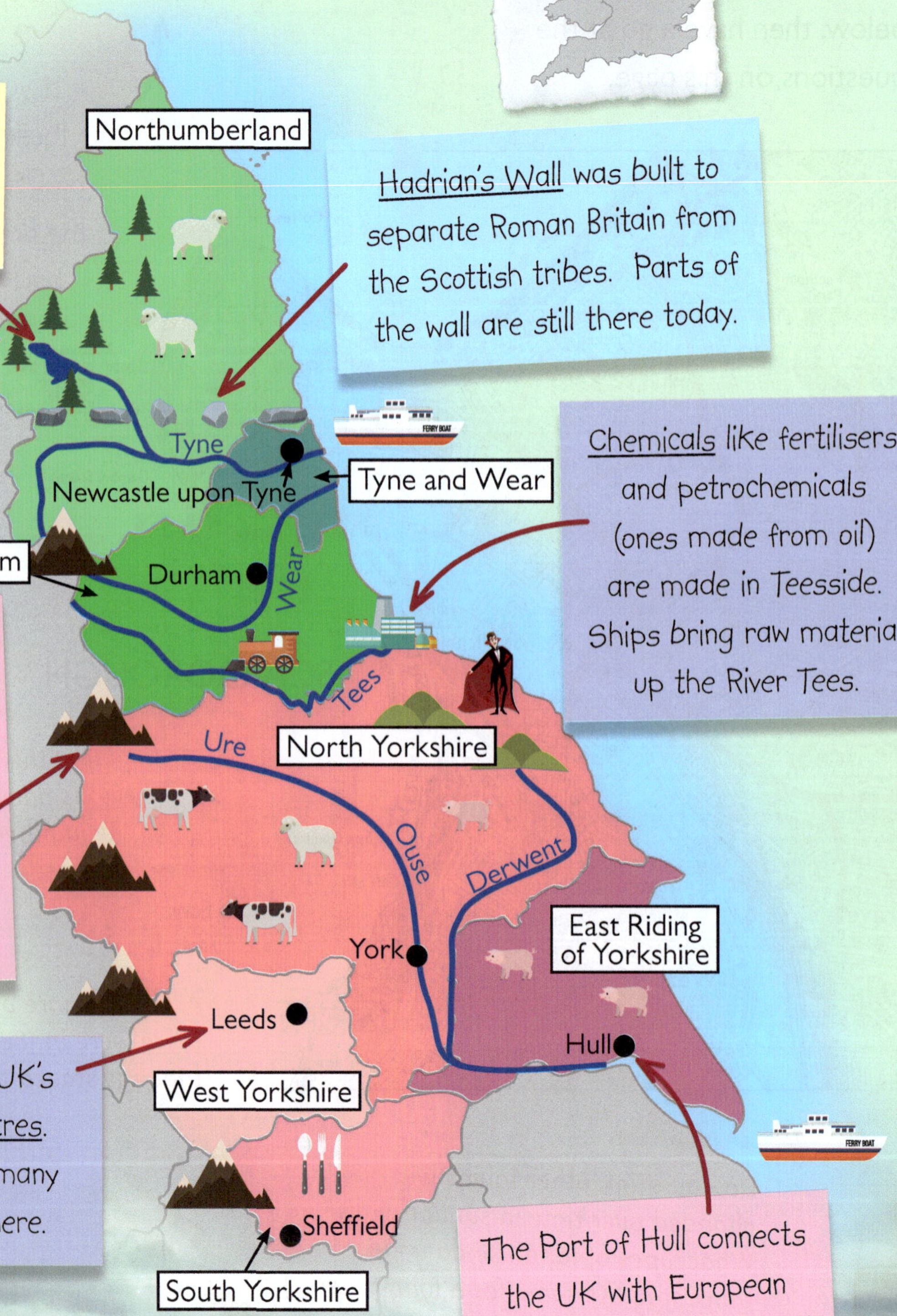

<u>Kielder Water</u> is a <u>reservoir</u> in England's largest <u>forest</u>.

Northumberland

<u>Hadrian's Wall</u> was built to separate Roman Britain from the Scottish tribes. Parts of the wall are still there today.

Tyne

Newcastle upon Tyne

Tyne and Wear

<u>Chemicals</u> like fertilisers and petrochemicals (ones made from oil) are made in Teesside. Ships bring raw material up the River Tees.

County Durham

Durham

Wear

The <u>Pennines</u> are a series of small <u>mountains</u> and <u>hills</u> that separate North Eastern England from the North West. They're often called 'the backbone of England'.

Tees

Ure

North Yorkshire

Ouse

Derwent

East Riding of Yorkshire

York

Leeds

West Yorkshire

Leeds is one of the UK's largest <u>financial centres</u>. The head offices of many banks are located here.

Hull

Sheffield

South Yorkshire

The Port of Hull connects the UK with European countries like <u>Belgium</u> and <u>the Netherlands</u>.

The <u>farmland</u> in these regions is mainly used for <u>sheep</u>, <u>pigs</u> and <u>cattle</u> rather than growing crops.

A shared past

The Romans built many forts in the north of England. Settlements then grew up around these forts. Here are two settlements in North Eastern England with Roman history.

Corbridge

Corbridge is a village in Northumberland. Around 2000 years ago, it was the site of a Roman <u>fort</u>, which then grew to a <u>market town</u>. Roman soldiers guarding Hadrian's Wall could get <u>food</u> and other <u>supplies</u> from here. The site was a good place for trade because it sat on an important <u>crossroads</u>.

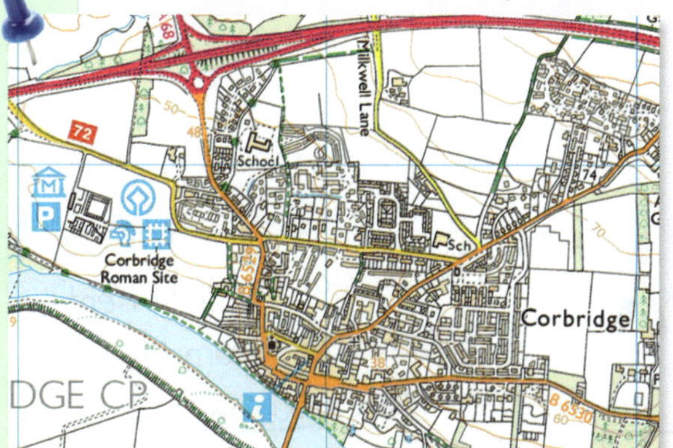

However, the town was abandoned when the Romans left Britain. Around 200 years later, <u>Saxons</u> built a small settlement by the original site, at a better place to cross the river. They took stones from the Roman fort to build their settlement. These days, Corbridge has a high street with <u>small shops</u> and <u>local businesses</u>.

York

The city of York was founded by the Romans in 71 AD. They built a <u>walled fortress</u> for the <u>military</u> on high ground beside the <u>River Ouse</u>. The rest of the city grew on the other side of the river. This is where non-military people like <u>traders</u> and <u>families</u> lived.

Today, the city centre is still surrounded by <u>walls</u> and it's packed with shops and tourist attractions. Most people live <u>outside the centre</u> on the other side of the walls.

Look at the two OS® maps on this page. What similarities and differences can you see between these two places?

Settlements usually start off for a reason...

York was built between two rivers — the Ouse and the Foss. The site was ideal as the rivers provided defence on both sides, and supplies could be transported to the city by boat.

South Eastern England

This corner of England includes counties with some of the largest populations and biggest economies in England.

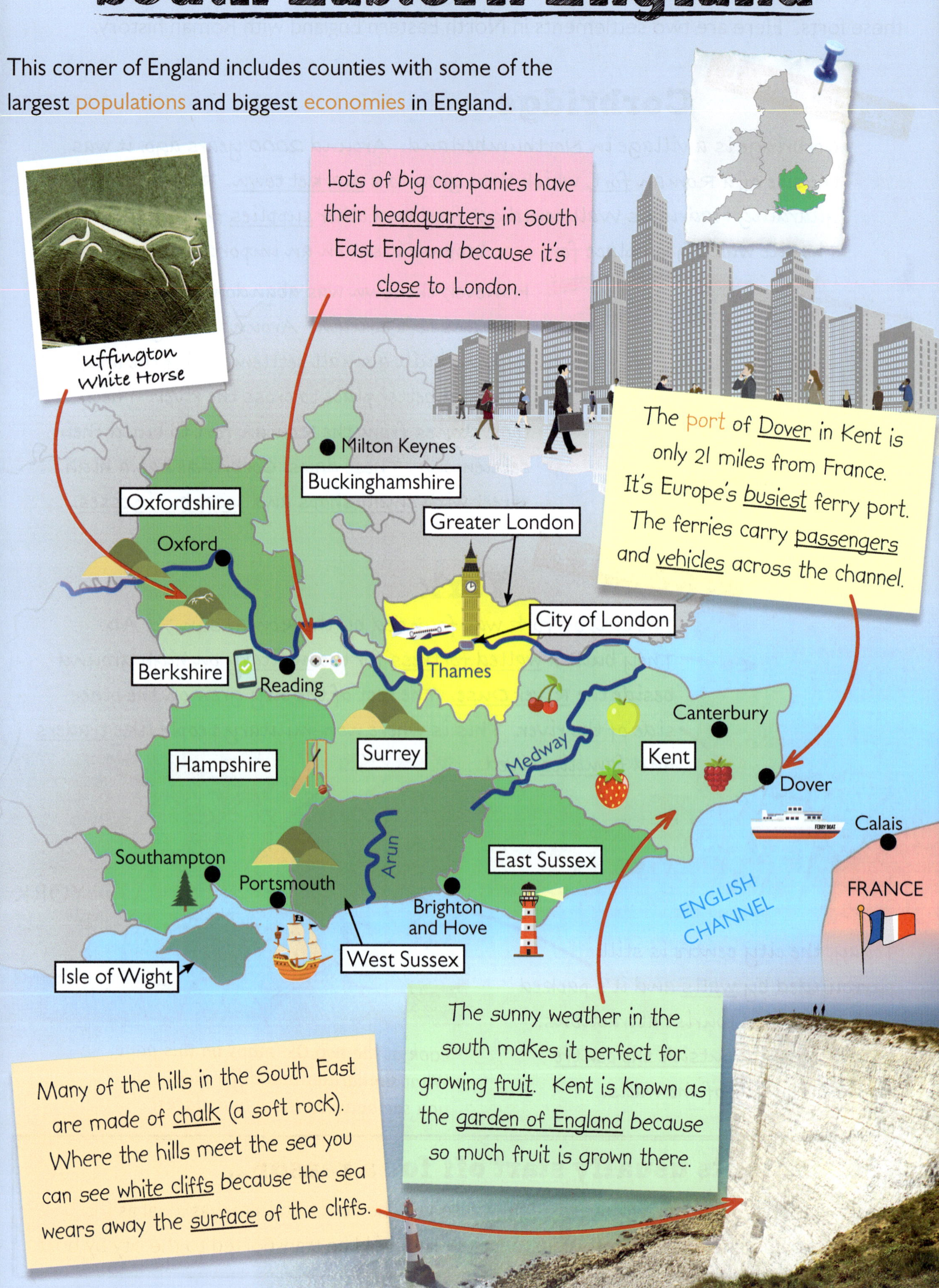

Naturally grown or carefully planned?

Land use changes all the time as populations grow and people's needs change. It often changes gradually over centuries, but it can sometimes change very quickly.

London

The city of London has grown slowly over many years. It began as the Roman settlement of Londinium around 2000 years ago. It was a very important port and trading centre. The first roads were built by the Romans and fanned out from the port. Over centuries, the city expanded in all directions — more roads were built and surrounding villages became part of the city itself.

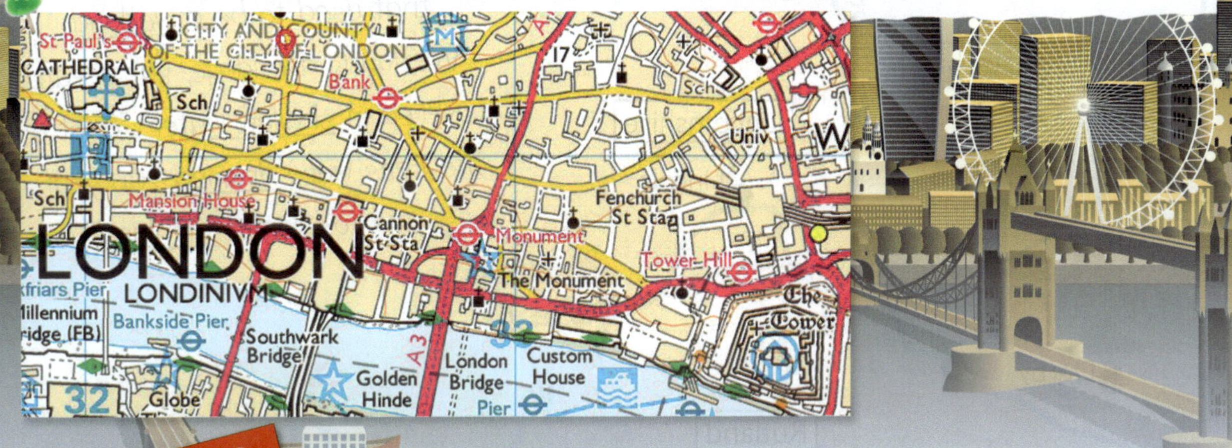

Milton Keynes

Milton Keynes is a new town, located about 50 miles from London. It was built in 1967 because there weren't enough houses for everyone in London. The area where it was built was previously farmland and small villages. The town was designed with roads in a grid pattern.

There are roundabouts where the roads cross to keep traffic moving smoothly through the town.

What else do you think the planners included when designing Milton Keynes?

Some not-so-new towns...

The idea of building new towns wasn't a new one in the 1960s. The first new towns were built after the Second World War to rehouse people whose homes had been bombed.

Eastern England

Eastern England is mostly <u>rural</u> and pretty <u>flat</u>, so there's a lot of <u>arable farming</u> here, growing <u>vegetables</u> and <u>cereals</u>.

Nottinghamshire is home to Sherwood Forest, where the legendary outlaw Robin Hood is said to have lived.

The Fens are an area of land that used to be a <u>wetland</u>. Wetlands are large, flat areas covered in <u>shallow water</u>. A lot of the Fens were <u>drained</u> 200 years ago to create <u>farmland</u>.

There is a lot of manufacturing in the East Midlands. <u>Trains</u>, <u>cars</u> and <u>jet engines</u> are built in Derby.

The Norfolk Broads are an area of <u>protected</u> <u>wetland</u>. They are home to many rare birds, plants and insects. Some of the <u>broads</u> (lakes) are also used for <u>sailing</u> and other <u>leisure activities</u>.

From hi-tech science to spuds

The <u>flat</u> land of Cambridgeshire makes it perfect for <u>arable farming</u>. However, the area around Cambridge is also home to a lot of companies in the hi-tech industry.

Hi-Tech Industry

Around the city of Cambridge there are several <u>science parks</u>, where lots of <u>hi-tech</u> companies are based. These do all sorts of things, from developing new <u>medicines</u> to making <u>programs</u> for computers.

This area is perfect for science parks because it's close to the university, where there's a lot of <u>research</u>, and there's also plenty of open space for <u>offices</u> and factories.

The science parks started growing in the <u>1970s</u>, <u>expanding</u> from the university. They employ many people from the university, who are <u>highly educated</u> and usually <u>highly paid</u>.

The area around Cambridge is nicknamed '<u>Silicon Fen</u>'. This is because it's a bit like 'Silicon Valley', the famous hi-tech area in California.

Fen Farming

The Fens hold some of the <u>best</u> agricultural land in England. The area used to be a <u>wetland</u>, so the soil is full of <u>dead</u> and <u>rotting</u> <u>plants</u> which put lots of <u>nutrients</u> into the soil. Because of this, the farmland is really <u>fertile</u>. Farms here grow <u>food crops</u>, such as potatoes, sugar beet and celery, as well as <u>flowers</u> like daffodils.

Thousands of people work in <u>farming</u> in Cambridgeshire. Jobs on farms are often <u>seasonal</u> and <u>low-paid</u>. Many workers come from <u>abroad</u> to work on the farms.

How many differences between these two industries can you think of?

Industries working together...

Some science park companies are working on digital products that can help farmers. Modern technology can make farming quicker and easier, for example, farmers can use a phone app to sow seeds in straight lines. Some devices can even drive a tractor!

South West England

The south west of England is almost <u>surrounded</u> by water.
An area of land like this is called a peninsula.
It's surrounded by the <u>Bristol Channel</u> to the north
and the <u>English Channel</u> to the south.

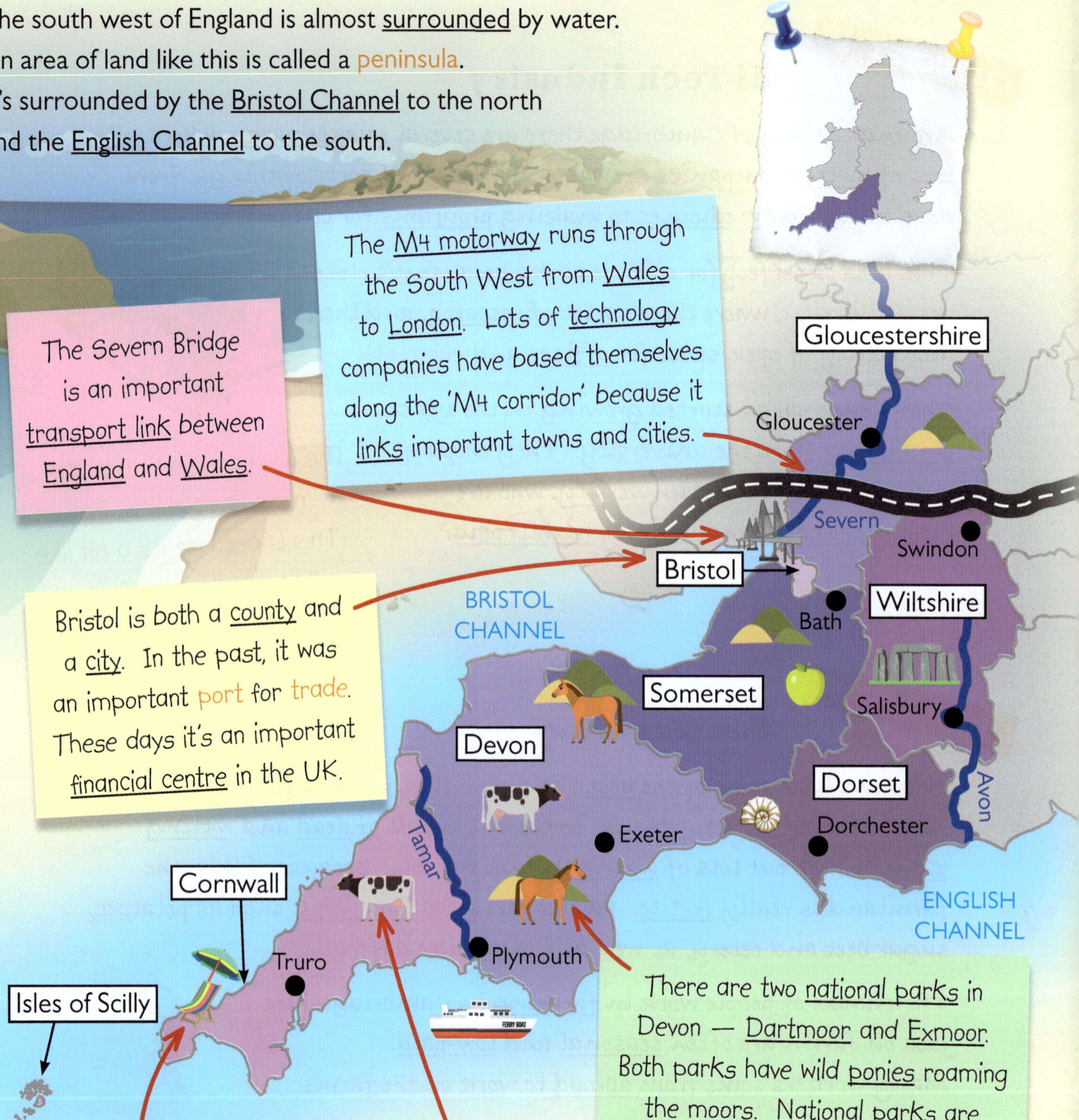

The <u>M4 motorway</u> runs through the South West from <u>Wales</u> to <u>London</u>. Lots of <u>technology</u> companies have based themselves along the 'M4 corridor' because it <u>links</u> important towns and cities.

The Severn Bridge is an important <u>transport link</u> between <u>England</u> and <u>Wales</u>.

Bristol is both a <u>county</u> and a <u>city</u>. In the past, it was an important port for trade. These days it's an important <u>financial centre</u> in the UK.

This region is one of the <u>warmest</u> in the UK because it's surrounded by the warmest <u>seas</u>. Cornwall is a popular <u>holiday destination</u> because of its warm and sunny weather.

There are two <u>national parks</u> in Devon — <u>Dartmoor</u> and <u>Exmoor</u>. Both parks have wild <u>ponies</u> roaming the moors. National parks are <u>protected</u> areas of nature.

<u>Dairy farming</u> is an important part of the industry in <u>Cornwall</u> and <u>Devon</u>. Both counties are famous for making <u>clotted cream</u>.

A rocky region

South West England is home to some impressive natural <u>rock formations</u> — both on the <u>coast</u> and <u>inland</u>. Many of these structures have been created by <u>water</u> over <u>millions</u> of years.

Durdle Door, Dorset

Durdle Door is a large <u>archway</u> made of <u>limestone</u> (a type of soft rock). It was formed by the waves crashing into the rocks over and over again for <u>millions</u> of years. The waves gradually <u>eroded</u> the weaker parts of rock until a <u>cave</u> formed. About 10 000 years ago, the waves broke through the other side of the cave to form an <u>arch</u>.

<u>Eroding</u> means gradually wearing something away, often over a long time.

Cheddar Gorge, Somerset

Cheddar Gorge was formed by <u>melting ice</u> during <u>glacial</u> (cold) periods over the last <u>million</u> years.

The melting ice formed a <u>river</u> that flowed over the limestone rocks. This gradually <u>eroded</u> the rocks downwards, carving a steep, narrow <u>valley</u>.

Dinosaur hunting...

Durdle Door is part of the Jurassic Coast — 95 miles of coast that stretches from Devon to Dorset. The coast is full of fossils that show us what dinosaurs and other animals were like 250 million years ago. You can even go hunting for fossils on Charmouth Beach.

Western England

From the remote <u>mountains</u> of Cumbria, through the big <u>cities</u> of Manchester and Birmingham to the <u>orchards</u> of Hereford, Western England has a lot of <u>variety</u>.

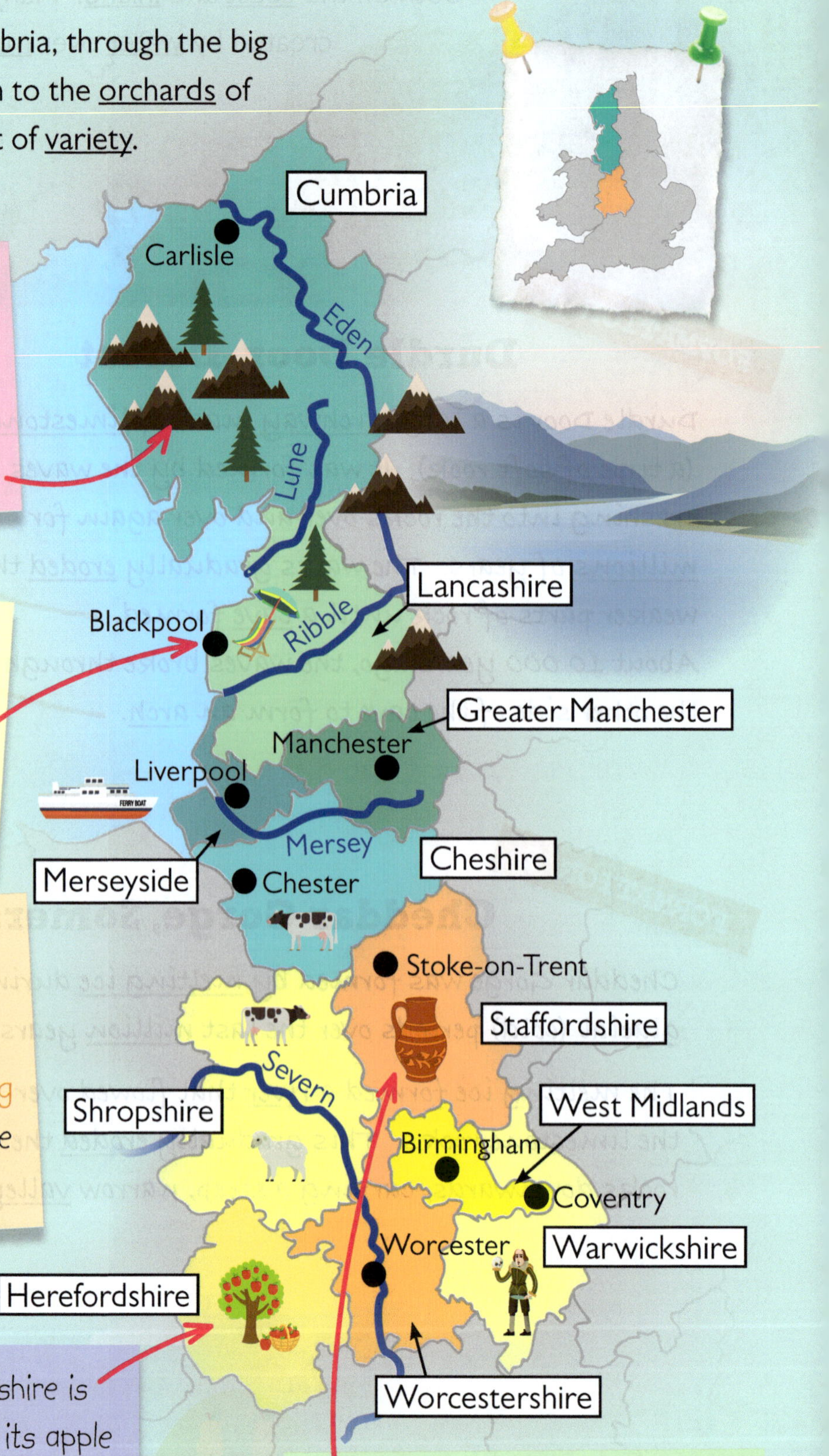

The <u>Lake District National Park</u> is in <u>Cumbria</u>. It's the <u>largest</u> national park in England. It's also home to England's tallest mountain — <u>Scafell Pike</u>.

<u>Blackpool</u> has been a popular <u>tourist resort</u> for around 200 years. People come to visit the <u>beach</u> and the <u>amusement park</u>.

The North West once had a large <u>textiles</u> industry, but it ended in the late 20th Century. There's still a lot of manufacturing here though, producing things like <u>aircraft</u> and <u>medicines</u>.

Herefordshire is famous for its apple and pear <u>orchards</u>.

<u>Pottery</u> is manufactured in Staffordshire because lots of <u>clay</u> and <u>coal</u> can be found nearby.

Have you been to any of the cities on this map?

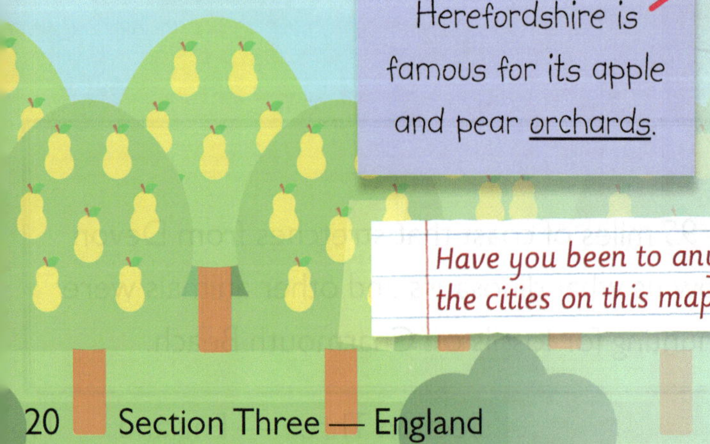

Waterways – then and now

The cities of Manchester, Liverpool and Birmingham were important centres of trade and industry during the Industrial Revolution. The quickest and cheapest way to transport raw materials and finished goods was by boat. This led to the rapid development of waterways to connect the cities and the coast, and docks to connect the UK to other countries. These connections still exist today, although they are not used in the same way. Here are two examples...

Liverpool Docks

Liverpool was one of the most important ports for the textile industry during the Industrial Revolution. Docks grew quickly in this area to support increased exports and imports. Cotton was imported from America to make cloth and clothing. This cloth was then exported from the UK to other countries.

As ships got bigger, docks also had to get bigger. Over the years, the old docks were abandoned as newer, larger docks were built. Recently, some of the old docks have been restored. They're now full of museums, restaurants, shops and hotels.

The Bridgewater Canal

The Bridgewater Canal was one of many canals built during the Industrial Revolution. It was part of a system of canals to transport coal from mines in the Lancashire countryside to sell in Manchester and Liverpool.

Canals were important for trade because the roads weren't suitable for heavy vehicles. Travelling by canal was quicker and large loads could be carried.

When the railways were built, the use of canals for transporting goods declined and many canals were abandoned. The Bridgewater Canal was one of the few that remained open, but it's now only used for leisure.

Over the last 50 years, lots more canals have been restored and reopened for leisure.

Moving on up...

The landscape has changed a lot since the Industrial Revolution. One reason is that technology has moved on. Now we have lorries and trains to transport goods.

Southern Scotland

Southern Scotland is an area with lots of lovely <u>countryside</u>.
It's got a bit of everything — <u>farmland</u>, <u>hills</u>, <u>beaches</u> and <u>forests</u>.

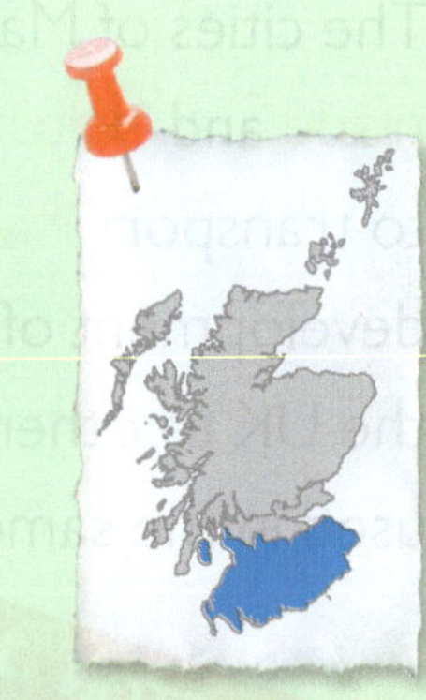

The <u>Isle of Arran</u> is part of North Ayrshire. It's a popular <u>tourist</u> destination with many beaches, walking routes and golf courses.

The <u>River Tweed</u> is famous for <u>fishing</u>. Lots of people visit the area to fish for <u>salmon</u>.

The <u>Cheviots</u> are a range of <u>hills</u> on the border of Scotland and England. It's a big <u>sheep farming</u> area — there's even a type of sheep called the <u>Cheviot</u>.

The <u>Galloway Forest Park</u> is a huge <u>forest</u> in Dumfries and Galloway. It's a <u>dark sky park</u> — that means it's a great place to go to look at the night sky because there is a low amount of <u>artificial light</u>.

Cheviot sheep

A breeze through the trees...

A lot of the <u>countryside</u> in Southern Scotland is made up of <u>low hills</u>.
Land like this is ideal for <u>planting forests</u> and <u>building wind farms</u>,
which is what two important industries in the area are based on.

Forestry

There are lots of <u>forests</u> in Southern Scotland. Some of them are natural, but many of them were <u>planted</u> to produce <u>timber</u> (wood). Growing timber brings <u>money</u> and <u>jobs</u> to the area.

Forests are really important for the UK's <u>biodiversity</u> (the <u>variety</u> of living things). Therefore, planted forests need to be <u>managed</u> so that they provide <u>habitats</u> for lots of species. There should be different <u>types</u> of tree to attract different sorts of wildlife. Also, the trees should be of different <u>ages</u>. One reason for this is that older trees often have <u>holes</u> in which <u>bats</u> can roost and certain types of <u>bird</u> can nest.

Wind Energy

A wind farm is an area covered by <u>wind turbines</u>. When the wind blows, the turbines <u>turn</u> and produce <u>electricity</u>.

Wind turbines <u>don't</u> release greenhouse gases and they may <u>reduce</u> the need to <u>burn fuels</u> that <u>do</u> release greenhouse gases, so they're good for the environment. And wind energy is renewable — so it won't <u>run out</u>.

But building wind farms does change the <u>look</u> of a place.
This can upset people who don't want an area to be <u>changed</u>.

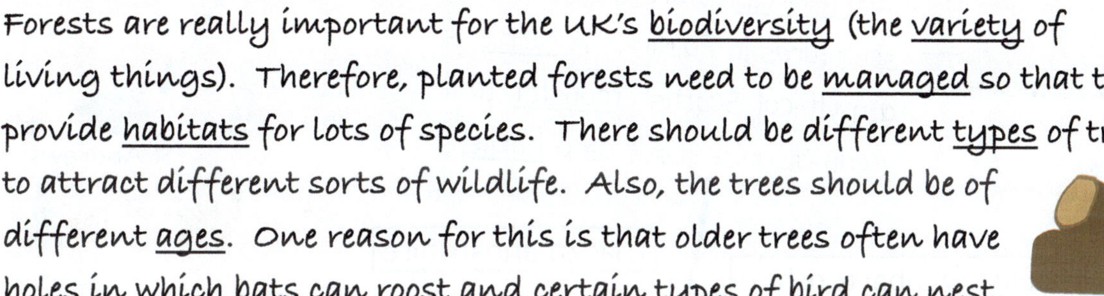

Ups and downs...

Forestry and wind energy are important industries, but they can both have an effect on the area around them. They need to be well-planned to try to keep everyone happy.

Central Scotland

Around <u>half</u> of Scotland's population live in Central Scotland.
It's <u>less hilly</u> than the rest of Scotland and includes some large urban areas.

Golf was invented in Scotland. The oldest golf course in the world is in <u>St Andrews</u>.

<u>The Kelpies</u> are giant steel sculptures in Falkirk. A <u>Kelpie</u> is a mythical Scottish <u>monster</u> that can disguise itself as a <u>horse</u>.

Whitelee Wind Farm is the biggest <u>onshore wind farm</u> in the UK. Most of Scotland's energy comes from <u>renewable sources</u> and most of that is from <u>wind power</u>.

The <u>Firth of Forth</u> is an estuary where the <u>River Forth</u> meets the sea. It's crossed by the famous <u>Forth Bridge</u>.

Millions of tourists visit Edinburgh every year. A world-famous attraction is the huge <u>Hogmanay</u> street party that takes place at New Year.

<u>Hogmanay</u> is the <u>Scots</u> word for <u>New Year's Eve</u>. Scots is a language spoken by some people in <u>Central</u> and <u>Southern</u> Scotland.

The perfect place for a city

Central Scotland is where you'll find Scotland's two <u>biggest cities</u> — <u>Edinburgh</u> and <u>Glasgow</u>. They're only about 40 miles apart, but each city formed for a completely different reason.

Edinburgh

Around the 11th century, <u>Edinburgh Castle</u> was built on top of <u>Castle Rock</u>, which is an <u>extinct volcano</u>. It's location made it the perfect spot from which to keep a look out for approaching <u>enemies</u> and to protect the people who lived around it. Because of this, Edinburgh grew into a busy town and eventually became the capital city of Scotland.

Today, Edinburgh is the home of the <u>Scottish Government</u> and the <u>Scottish Parliament</u>. It's not an <u>industrial</u> city, but instead it's famous for <u>banking</u>, <u>computing</u> and <u>tourism</u>.

Glasgow

People have lived around the River Clyde since <u>Roman</u> times, but it was during the 18th and 19th centuries that Glasgow grew into an <u>industrial city</u>. Its industries included <u>coal mining</u> and <u>textile manufacture</u>, but it was most famous for shipbuilding. It was also an important port city for trade between the UK and the USA, because the River Clyde gives easy access to the <u>Atlantic Ocean</u>.

A lot of Glasgow's heavy industry has now gone. Today, it's a centre for newer industries like <u>aerospace engineering</u>.

Ever evolving...

Both cities have changed a lot since they were founded. Today, Edinburgh Castle is a tourist attraction and museum. The area around the River Clyde is now mostly used for leisure — there are many shops, cinemas, hotels and museums along the river in Glasgow.

Northern Scotland

Northern Scotland is a land of <u>mountains</u>, <u>islands</u> and <u>lochs</u> (lakes).
It takes up about <u>half of the area</u> of Scotland, but only
a <u>quarter</u> of the population live there.

There are about 800 <u>islands</u> around Northern Scotland, but fewer than 100 of them are <u>inhabited</u>. <u>Tourism</u>, <u>fishing</u> and <u>weaving</u> are important industries on the islands.

Would you like to live on a small island?

Loch Ness is a deep <u>lake</u> in the Highlands where the legendary Loch Ness Monster is said to live.

Ben Nevis is the <u>highest mountain</u> in the UK. It's 1345 m high.

Northern Scotland is divided by the <u>Great Glen</u> — a huge <u>valley</u> formed by a <u>fault line</u> (a long crack in the Earth's crust).

The <u>Caledonian Canal</u> is a canal that cuts through the <u>Great Glen</u>. It was built in the 1800s as a <u>quicker</u> and <u>safer</u> way to sail from one side of Scotland to the other. Before then, people had to sail around the north coast.

Big mountains and big machines

The economy of Northern Scotland is based on two very different industries — tourism and extraction of oil and gas. Both make the most of the area's natural resources. Tourists come to visit the mountains, and the oil and gas industry relies on materials found underground.

Tourism

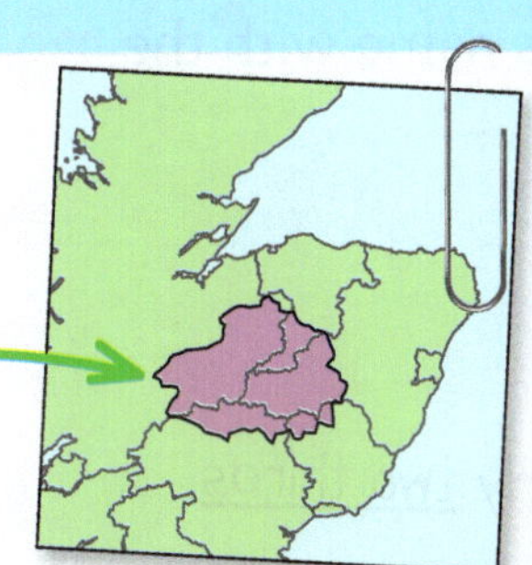

The Cairngorms are a mountain range in Northern Scotland. The Cairngorm area became a National Park in 2003.

Lots of tourists visit the area to enjoy the mountains, going walking in summer and skiing in winter. They also come to see rare birds and animals, like pine martens and crossbills.

These visitors spend money in local businesses, like shops and hotels. This also creates jobs, as people are needed to work in these businesses.

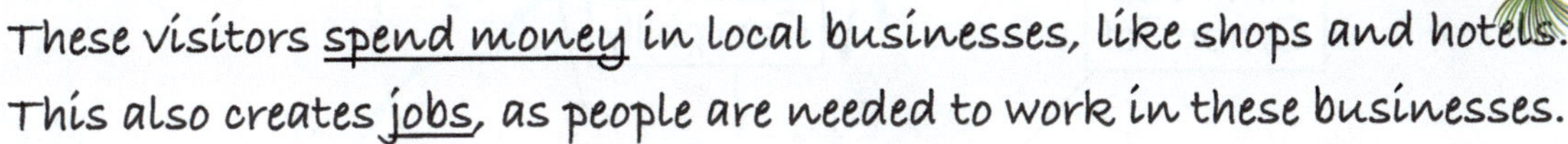

Oil and Natural Gas

There are lots of oil rigs off the east coast of Scotland. Oil rigs are huge platforms built out at sea. They drill down into the sea bed and pump out oil and natural gas from under the sea.

Oil and natural gas are fuels. They have lots of uses — many houses have heating systems that use natural gas, and petrol is made from oil.

The oil industry brings lots of money and jobs to Northern Scotland — especially to Aberdeen, where lots of people work as engineers, scientists and technicians on the oil rigs. Oil companies also have huge offices in Aberdeen, which employ accountants, lawyers and businesspeople.

Money spinners...

It might surprise you that two such different industries carry on so close to each other, but both industries generate thousands of jobs and billions of pounds for Scotland.

South Wales

South Wales is the <u>busiest</u> and most <u>industrial</u> part of Wales. It's split into twelve <u>principal areas</u>. The principal area of <u>Cardiff</u> shares its name with the capital city of Wales.

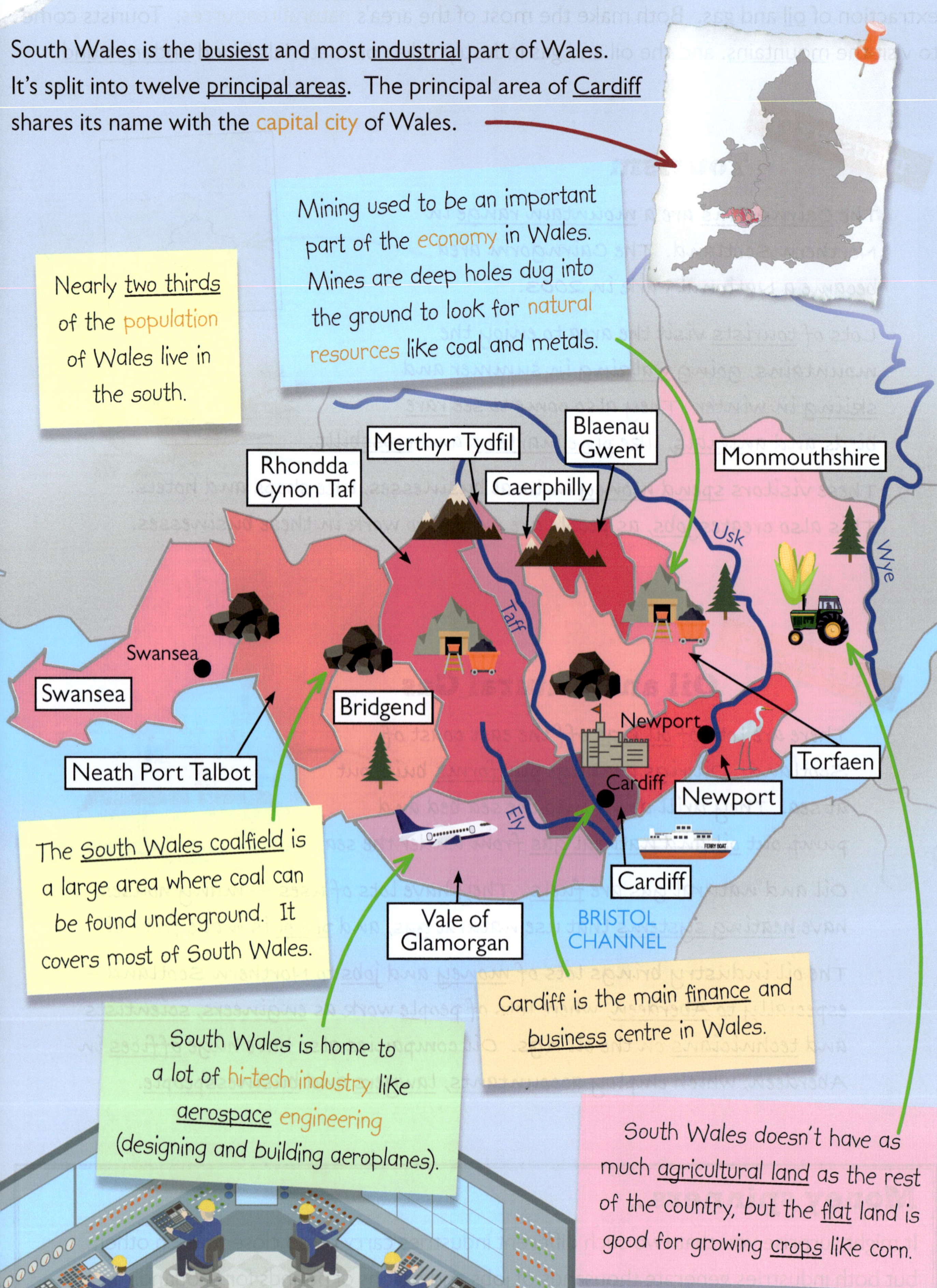

A new lease of life

Coal mining used to be the <u>main industry</u> in South Wales, but the demand for coal <u>decreased</u> in the mid 1900s. Places that used to be important for the coal industry were left <u>empty</u> because they were no longer needed, but now they've been <u>renovated</u> in different ways.

LOCATION 1 Cardiff Bay

Cardiff Bay was once one of the busiest ports in the world, full of huge ships transporting coal all over the world. Since the coal industry <u>declined</u>, the area became <u>neglected</u> and <u>run down</u>.

The government wanted to <u>attract</u> people back to work and live in the docks area. It was decided that the bay's <u>tidal</u> nature (which meant <u>flat, muddy land</u> could be seen at <u>low tide</u>) made the area <u>unattractive</u>. A huge dam called a <u>barrage</u> was built which created a <u>lake</u> in the bay.

The change did encourage <u>businesses</u> to move to the area. Now there are many <u>shops</u>, <u>restaurants</u> and <u>tourist attractions</u>, as well as <u>flats</u> and <u>offices</u>.

Can you think of any reasons why building the barrage might have been a bad idea?

LOCATION 2 Big Pit

<u>Big Pit</u> was a <u>coal mine</u> in the town of Blaenavon in Torfaen. It closed in 1980, but was reopened as a <u>museum</u> three years later.

The buildings and underground tunnels have been mostly <u>kept as they were</u> when it was a working mine. Visitors can go into the mines and see what <u>life was like</u> for the miners who worked down there.

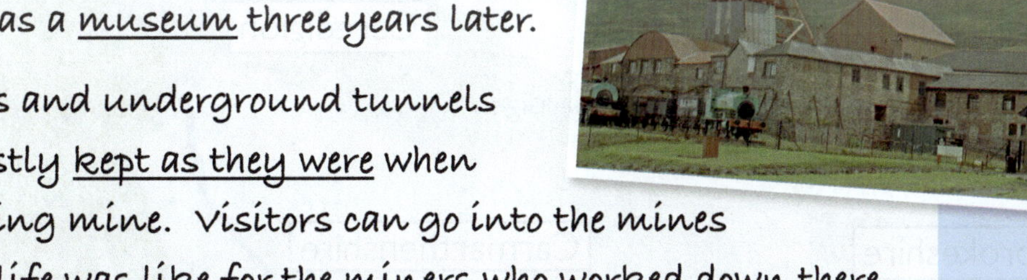

Eat your vegetables...

Did you know the national emblem (symbol) of Wales is a leek? Leeks were important in the past for many reasons. In ancient times, some Welsh people thought leeks could help cure colds, get rid of pain and even help you tell the future. That's one magic veggie.

Central & Northern Wales

Central and Northern Wales are <u>mountainous</u> areas.
There's not as much industry as there is in the South.

Central Wales and Northern Wales
are made up of ten <u>principal areas</u>.

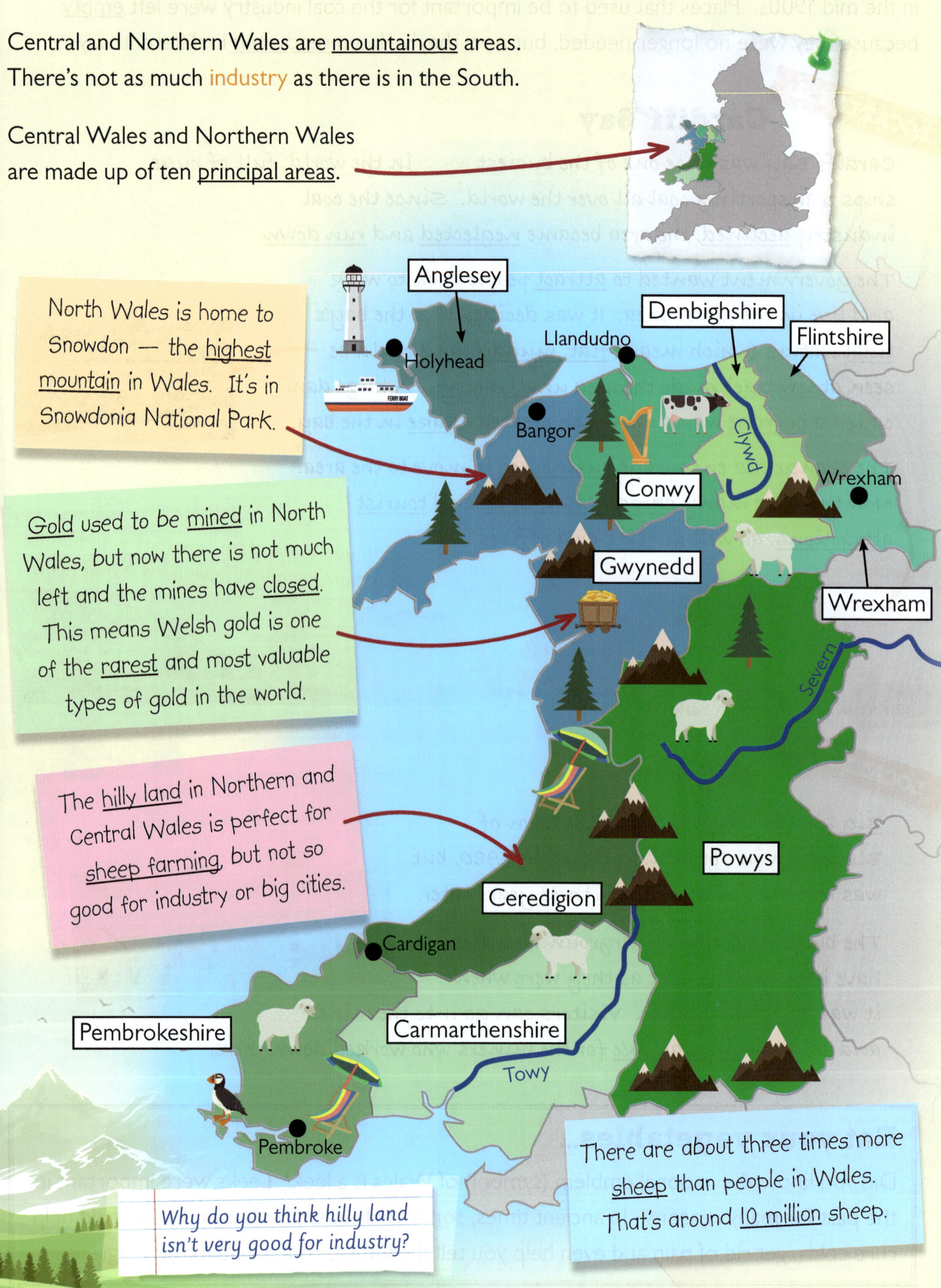

North Wales is home to
Snowdon — the <u>highest</u>
<u>mountain</u> in Wales. It's in
Snowdonia National Park.

<u>Gold</u> used to be <u>mined</u> in North
Wales, but now there is not much
left and the mines have <u>closed</u>.
This means Welsh gold is one
of the <u>rarest</u> and most valuable
types of gold in the world.

The <u>hilly land</u> in Northern and
Central Wales is perfect for
<u>sheep farming</u>, but not so
good for industry or big cities.

There are about three times more
<u>sheep</u> than people in Wales.
That's around <u>10 million</u> sheep.

*Why do you think hilly land
isn't very good for industry?*

From peaks to beaches

North Wales has a wide range of <u>physical features</u>, from <u>mountain ranges</u> to <u>coastlines</u>. Even though they look very different, both of these landscapes were created over thousands of years by <u>erosion</u> (when the land is gradually <u>worn away</u> by ice, water or wind).

Mountains and valleys

<u>Snowdonia National Park</u> covers most of Gwynedd and part of Conwy. Much of the landscape of Snowdonia was <u>carved out</u> by ice around 18 000 years ago.

Back then, almost all of the UK was covered in <u>ice sheets</u> and <u>glaciers</u>. Glaciers are huge masses of <u>ice</u> that move very <u>slowly</u> downhill. Rocks that are frozen to the base and sides of the glacier grind against the rocks on the ground, <u>eroding</u> the land as the glacier moves. The glacier also <u>pulls</u> more rocks out of the ground as it goes.

Over thousands of years, glaciers in Snowdonia carved out huge <u>valleys</u>, <u>ridges</u> and <u>lakes</u> and even shaped the <u>mountains</u>.

Headlands and bays

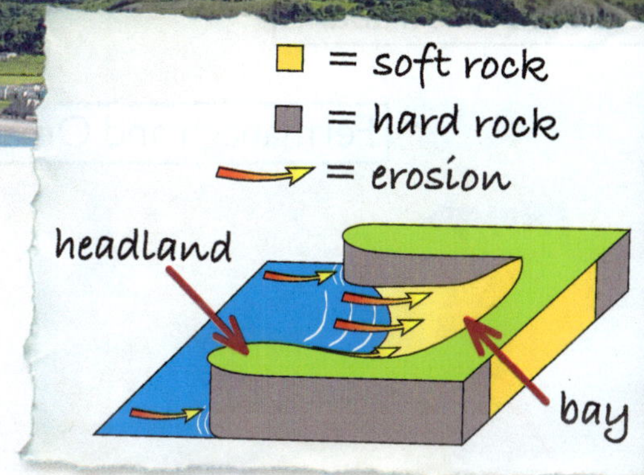

Headlands and bays are <u>coastal landforms</u> that are formed where the coast is made up of <u>bands</u> of <u>soft</u> and <u>hard</u> rock.

The waves <u>erode</u> the soft rock more <u>quickly</u> than the hard rock. This leaves the hard rock <u>sticking out</u> into the sea. The bits sticking out are called headlands. The gap between them, where the soft rock has been worn away, is a bay.

The <u>Great Orme</u> is a headland near the <u>coastal town</u> of <u>Llandudno</u> in Conwy.

Could you repeat that, please?

The longest place name in the UK belongs to a village on the Welsh island of Anglesey called <u>Llanfairpwllgwyngyllgogerychwyrndrobwllllantysiliogogogoch</u>. It's a bit of a mouthful, so people usually just shorten it to Llanfair PG (pronounced hlan-vire PG).

Northern Ireland

Northern Ireland has a mixture of large rural areas and urban areas with a lot of industry. It's split into eleven districts.

The Giant's Causeway is an area of thousands of hexagonal (six-sided) columns of rock that were created when a volcano erupted millions of years ago.

Giant's Causeway, County Antrim

Lough Neagh is the largest lake in the UK by area.

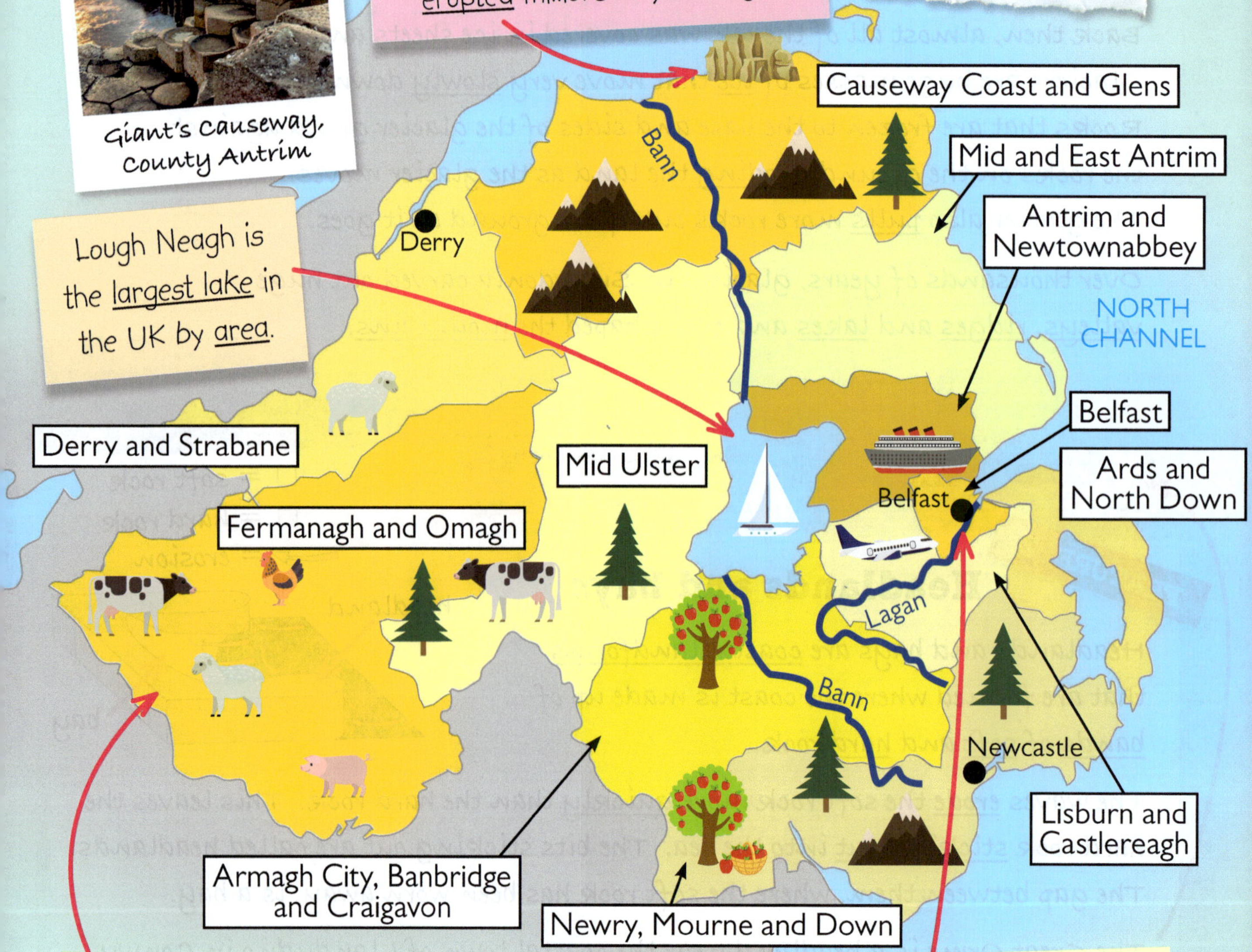

Three quarters of the countryside in Northern Ireland is used as farmland. Most of it is used for grazing cattle and sheep but some crops are grown here too.

Belfast's position on the River Lagan made it an important port and centre for trade. In the late 1800s, the city had one of the largest shipyards in the world. The famous ship 'Titanic' was built in Belfast. However, these days the shipyard is closed.

Times are changing

The most important economic activities of an area can <u>change</u> over time. In the past, Northern Ireland had an economy based on manufacturing and heavy industry — Belfast was particularly famous for making <u>ropes</u> and <u>fabrics</u>, as well as <u>ships</u>. These days, those industries still exist but other economic activities are growing...

ACTIVITY 1

Financial Technology

Financial technology is a new type of service industry. It uses <u>computer programs</u> to make <u>financial services</u> (such as banking) easier for people to use. It includes technology that allows people to pay for things using their <u>smartphone</u>, as well as programs that <u>protect</u> people from having their money stolen online. Belfast has become a <u>world centre</u> for financial technology companies and the number of <u>jobs</u> in this area is <u>growing rapidly</u>.

ACTIVITY 2

Tourism

Until the late <u>1990s</u>, <u>conflict</u> in Northern Ireland (known as the Troubles) meant that there wasn't much <u>tourism</u> in the country. This is because many people felt it was too <u>dangerous</u> to travel there. However, since the Troubles ended, tourism has been <u>growing</u>.

Coastal towns like <u>Newcastle</u> in County Down have become popular tourist destinations because of their beautiful <u>beaches</u>. Tourists also come to see the country's many <u>castles</u>, the <u>Giant's Causeway</u> and the <u>Titanic Belfast</u> (a visitor attraction built on the old Belfast shipyard).

> Tourism can have both positive and negative effects on an area. How many can you think of?

Big builders...

According to legend, the Giant's Causeway is the remains of a huge road built by a giant. He wanted to cross the sea to Scotland, where another giant had challenged him to a fight. There are similar columns in Scotland, which are said to be the other end of the road.

Where Do You Live?

People live in different types of settlements, from huge cities to tiny hamlets.
Different types of settlement have different kinds of houses, services and things to do.

Country life

Villages are small settlements. They have a few houses, shops and services. They usually have a church and maybe a primary school. They are often surrounded by lots of fields and trees.
Hamlets are even smaller than villages and are made up of often only a few houses.

I'm Ben and I live in a village. My house is quite old and it has a big garden. There's only one little shop here, but there are lots of places to play outside. I go to school in the village just now, but I'll go to secondary school in a nearby town.

A bit of everything

Towns can be home to tens of thousands of people. They have lots of houses and they might have shopping centres, supermarkets, hospitals, secondary schools and railway stations.
People who work in towns tend to live locally.

My name's Jana. I live in a town. I like it here because there's lots to do, but it's not as busy as a city. There are a few busy roads but it's mostly quiet streets with houses. There are lots of parks where I can take my dog for a walk and play with my friends.

© Crown copyright (2019) OS 100034841

Bright lights, big city

Cities have the same things as towns but loads more of them. They often also have a
<u>cathedral</u> and a <u>university</u>. You can read more about what <u>services</u> you can find in a city on
page 6. In cities, people often live in blocks of <u>flats</u>. People who <u>work</u> in cities often live
<u>outside</u> the city centre and <u>travel</u> in to work.

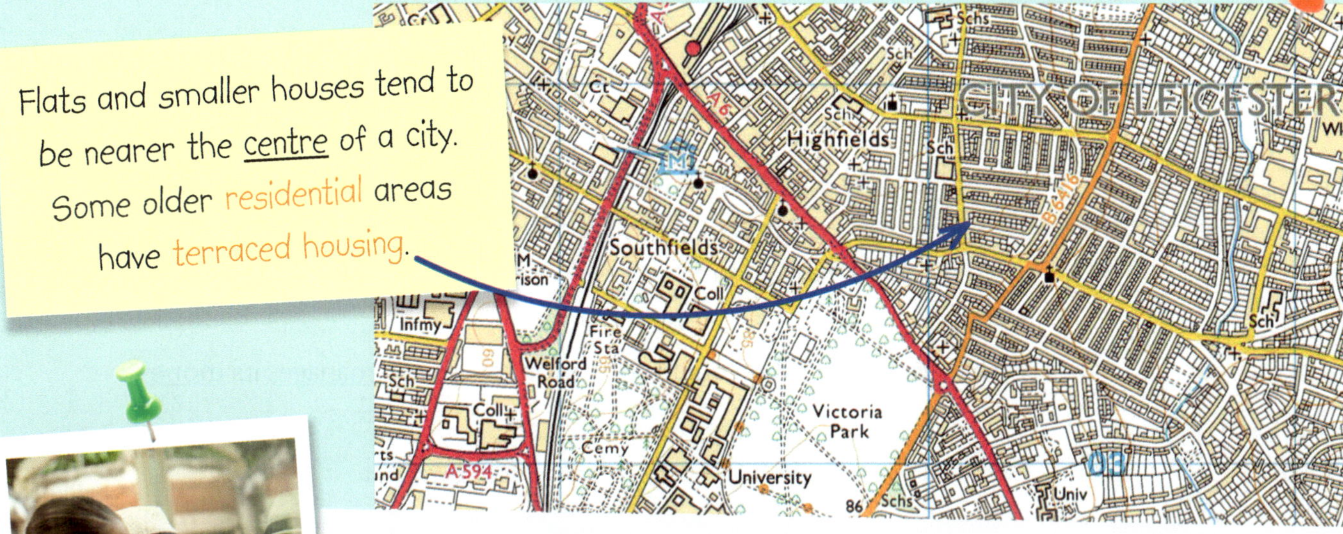

Flats and smaller houses tend to be nearer the <u>centre</u> of a city. Some older residential areas have terraced housing.

Hi. My name's Farah and I live in a city. I live in a flat on the
fifth floor of a really tall building. It's usually really busy
here and there's lots of traffic. There are also lots of shops and
things to do nearby. I like going to the cinema and the zoo
with my big sister and my dad at the weekend.

What about you?

Think about where <u>you</u> live. Try answering some of these questions to get you started...

STUDY YOUR SETTLEMENT

Homes: What are the houses like? Are they big or small? Old or new?
Are there many flats?

Services: What kinds of services are nearby? Is there a police station?
What about a doctor's surgery?

Things to do: Are there any fun things to do where you live?
Is there a cinema, a zoo, parks or a swimming pool?

Transport: Is there a train station or a bus station where you live?

The biggest of all...

Megacities are cities with more than 10 million people living in them. There are currently
37 megacities in the world, including New York and Tokyo, but there are none in the UK.

Glossary

agriculture	Another word for farming.
arable farming	Growing crops.
capital city	A city where the government of a country is based.
cattle farming	Rearing cows for dairy products and for meat.
economic activity	How people make money.
economy	The system of how a country or region makes and manages its money.
estuary	The really wide part of a river where it joins the sea.
exports	Goods that are sent to another country to sell.
factory	Where products (like cars, clothes, etc) are made.
government	A group of people that runs a country.
greenhouse gas	A gas in the atmosphere that traps heat from the Sun. Increasing the amount of greenhouse gases means that too much heat is trapped.
heavy industry	A type of industry that uses large and heavy machinery or makes large and heavy products e.g. mining, shipbuilding and building wind turbines.
hi-tech industry	Industry that involves making electronics and medicines.
imports	Goods that are brought in from another country to sell.
Industrial Revolution	A period of history when lots of factories were built, and huge numbers of people moved from rural to urban areas.
industry	An economic activity that involves collecting raw materials (like coal) or making products in factories.
land use	What people do with an area of land.
manufacturing	Industry that involves making products in factories.

natural resources	Resources found in nature that we can use. Fuel, food, minerals and water are natural resources.
new town	A town that is carefully planned and built in an undeveloped area.
peninsula	A piece of land that's almost completely surrounded by water.
population	The number of people who live in a particular place.
port	A place where ships can load and unload people and goods.
raw material	A material that is found in nature like coal, minerals, metals, wood or crops. Raw materials are usually turned into other things.
renewable (energy)	Energy that comes from a source that won't run out, like wind, the Sun or ocean tides.
reservoir	A natural or man-made lake that is used as a water source.
residential	An area that's made for people to live in.
resource	Things like food, fuel, metals and building materials that people use.
rural area	An area that doesn't have lots of buildings, like the countryside.
services / service industry	Things the public needs, like doctors, shops, banks and public transport.
settlement	A place where people live.
shipbuilding	A type of heavy industry that involves designing and building ships.
terraced housing	A row of several houses joined together.
The Troubles	A time of political conflict in Northern Ireland. The country was divided between people who wanted to be part of the UK and those who didn't. This caused a lot of violence and riots. This conflict lasted almost 30 years.
trade / trading	Buying or selling goods or services.
urban area	An area that is a town or city.

Acknowledgements

Cover photo: © iStock / Getty Images Plus / Getty Images.

Some paragraphs in this book are based on real-life events. However, some situations, characters and dialogue have been changed or invented for dramatic purposes — any similarity to a person, living or deceased, in these areas is merely coincidence.

Map extracts on pages 7, 11, 13, 15, 34 & 35 reproduced with permission from Ordnance Survey © Crown copyright (2019) OS 100034841.

Graphics used through this book: (push pin) © iStock.com/blackred. (lined paper) © iStock.com/subjug. (torn paper) © iStock.com/ Tolga TEZCAN.

Section One — The United Kingdom
p2 (Cardiff castle) © Giuseppe Ramos/Alamy Stock Vector. p3 (UK satellite image) © Universal Images Group North America LLC/ Alamy Stock Photo. p4 (national assembly for Wales) © Chris Howes/Wild Places Photography/Alamy Stock Photo.

Section Two — Land Use in the UK
p7 (Birmingham airport) © a-plus image bank/Alamy Stock Photo. p8 (tractor) © iStock.com/filo. p8 (autumn) © iStock.com/LEOcrafts. p10 (Scarborough promenade) © iStock.com/duncan1890.

Section Three — England
p13 (Roman York) Historic England / Mary Evans. p14 (Uffington white horse) USGS/NOSA.

Section Four — Scotland
p24 (Grangemouth - The Kelpies) © Colin Smith Licensed for re-use under the Creative Commons Attribution-ShareAlike 2.0 Generic (CC BY-SA 2.0) https://creativecommons.org/licenses/by-sa/2.0/.

Section Five — Wales and Northern Ireland
p29 view of the National Coal Museum by Nessy-Pic, Licensed under the Creative Commons Attribution-Share Alike 3.0 Unported license. https://creativecommons.org/licenses/by-sa/3.0/deed.en. p29 Cardiff Bay by Ben Salter licensed under the Creative Commons Attribution 2.0 Generic license https://creativecommons.org/licenses/by/2.0/deed.en.

Inside Cover
(old blank paper) © iStock.com/tomograf. (OS map symbols) © Crown copyright and database rights (2019) OS 100034841.